BEI GRIN MACHT SICH IHR WISSEN BEZAHLT

- Wir veröffentlichen Ihre Hausarbeit, Bachelor- und Masterarbeit

- Ihr eigenes eBook und Buch - weltweit in allen wichtigen Shops

- Verdienen Sie an jedem Verkauf

Jetzt bei www.GRIN.com hochladen und kostenlos publizieren

Bibliografische Information der Deutschen Nationalbibliothek:

Die Deutsche Bibliothek verzeichnet diese Publikation in der Deutschen Nationalbibliografie; detaillierte bibliografische Daten sind im Internet über http://dnb.d-nb.de/ abrufbar.

Dieses Werk sowie alle darin enthaltenen einzelnen Beiträge und Abbildungen sind urheberrechtlich geschützt. Jede Verwertung, die nicht ausdrücklich vom Urheberrechtsschutz zugelassen ist, bedarf der vorherigen Zustimmung des Verlages. Das gilt insbesondere für Vervielfältigungen, Bearbeitungen, Übersetzungen, Mikroverfilmungen, Auswertungen durch Datenbanken und für die Einspeicherung und Verarbeitung in elektronische Systeme. Alle Rechte, auch die des auszugsweisen Nachdrucks, der fotomechanischen Wiedergabe (einschließlich Mikrokopie) sowie der Auswertung durch Datenbanken oder ähnliche Einrichtungen, vorbehalten.

Impressum:

Copyright © 2014 GRIN Verlag
Druck und Bindung: Books on Demand GmbH, Norderstedt Germany
ISBN: 9783668715813

Dieses Buch bei GRIN:

https://www.grin.com/document/427435

J. J.

The Differences between Humans and Androids in Philip K. Dick's "Do Androids Dream of Electric Sheep?"

GRIN Verlag

GRIN - Your knowledge has value

Der GRIN Verlag publiziert seit 1998 wissenschaftliche Arbeiten von Studenten, Hochschullehrern und anderen Akademikern als eBook und gedrucktes Buch. Die Verlagswebsite www.grin.com ist die ideale Plattform zur Veröffentlichung von Hausarbeiten, Abschlussarbeiten, wissenschaftlichen Aufsätzen, Dissertationen und Fachbüchern.

Besuchen Sie uns im Internet:

http://www.grin.com/

http://www.facebook.com/grincom

http://www.twitter.com/grin_com

Universität Trier

Anglistik

LIT 401: Classics of American Science Fiction

The Differences between Humans and Androids in Philip K. Dick's *Do Androids Dream of Electric Sheep?*

J. J.

Degree Program: Bachelor of Education

Table of contents:

1. Introduction 3
2. The Differences between Androids and Human Beings: 3
    2.1 Empathy 4
    2.2 The Role of Animals: 6
3. Conclusion 8
Bibliography 9

1. Introduction:

The characters in Philip K. Dick´s novel *Do Androids Dream of Electric Sheep?* are either humans or androids, these androids are inferior to human beings and among the humans there are bounty hunters whose task it is to kill the androids (Jabbar 2012). The androids intend to be like human beings by the way the live and by behaving like humans (Galvan 1997, 418). It is interesting to examine what distinguishes the androids in the novel from human beings and if these distinctions are clear or if there are some contradictions or problems when it comes to distinguishing between androids and humans. First of all, this paper will investigate the differences between androids and human beings according to Dick´s novel in general and then it will focus on empathy which plays an important role in the story. It will be dealt with general definitions of empathy and the question if empathy is really a distinguishing factor or if androids are also able to feel empathy to a certain extent. Furthermore, the paper will concentrate on the role of animals for human beings in general and on the role animals play for the human beings in the novel.

2. The Differences between Androids and Human Beings:

The androids in the novel are constructed the way they look like real human beings, but they are actually not (Bhabha 1994, 86). Nevertheless, they want to be like humans:

> "It is the desire for a reformed, recognizable other, as a subject of a difference that is almost the same, but not quite, which is to say that the discourse of mimicry is constructed around an ambivalence."(Bhabha 1994, 86).

They spend time with other humans and have jobs in order to feel more human, like J.R. Isidore does: "You have to be with other people, he thought. In order to live at all." (Dick 2007, 178). So the androids are very much like humans and according to Dick their intention is not to deceive humans for any reason, they just live like human beings do and therefore "…they are, in many ways, actually human already…" (Jabbar 2012).One obvious factor that distinguishes the androids from humans is that they are artificially created and not born, furthermore they do not grow older and they do not die the way humans die: " Rachel: We´re not born, we don´t grow up; instead of dying from illness or old age we wear out like ants." (Dick 2007, 168). Apart from that, androids do not live as long as humans due to a problem with their cell replacement; which is exemplified in a conversation between Rick Deckard and the android Rachel Rosen (Dick 2007, 169). The type of androids that Rachel belongs to only live about four years, whereas most humans grow a lot older of course (Dick, 1968, 170). Although the androids in the novel do not grow up like humans do, they have memories, for instance, about their childhood, but these memories are not real, whereas the memories of humans are: "Only androids show up with false memory systems, it´s been found ineffective in humans." (Dick 2007, 110).There are also androids that are more intelligent than others, namely the androids with the Nexus 6 brain unit, but independent of their intelligence, the androids cannot understand Mercerism, the religion the humans in the novel believe in, and the androids are also not aware of the importance of this religion and how people are connected by Mercerism (Dick 2007, 25/26). Apart from the android´s lack of understanding Mercerism, the important role that animals play for humans,as well as, empathy are crucial factors when it comes to distinguishing androids from human beings. In the following, it will be dealt the role of animals and with empathy in detail and with the question if these two factors do really distinguish androids from humans or not.

2.1 Empathy

According to the Oxford Dictionary and the Oxford Advanced Learner´s Dictionary, empathy derived from the Greek term "empatheia" and means "the ability to understand another person´s feelings, experience, etc.", which means that one is able to put oneself in the position of someone. Feeling empathy for someone might be easier if one already had a likewise experience and knows how the person must feel after a certain occasion (Williams, 2003). Huit (2009), states that there is a difference between empathy and sympathy; empathy means "feeling as someone" while sympathy means "feeling for someone" (Huit 2009). When people feel empathy for someone it has more to do with themselves than feeling sympathy for someone, that is because when they feel empathy they refer to a part of themselves that has felt the same as the person they are feeling empathy for does in that moment (Matthews 2013). Compared to empathy, feeling sympathy for someone dissociates one more from oneself because the focus is more on something only the other person has experienced and that does not have to do very much with oneself (Matthews 2013).

In the novel, empathy is also a very important factor when it comes to distinguishing between real human beings and androids. Bounty hunters like Rick Deckard conduct the Voigt-

Kampff- Empathy Test in order to find out if the test taker is a human being or an android (Jabbar 2012). In this Voigt-Kampff-Empathy Test the interviewees have to react to some social situations very quickly and it is tested if they show empathy or not (Dick 2007, 41). Most of the situations that are given to the interviewees in the empathy test deal with cruelty towards animals which should prove that humans show empathy towards animals whereas androids do not (Dick 2007, 41). Furthermore, it is said in the novel that the androids can neither feel empathy for humans nor for other androids (Galvan 1997, 414):

> " `An android` he said, doesn´t care what happens to another android. That´s some of the indications we are looking for." (Dick 2007, 88).

So, the androids in the novel are defined as humanoid robots that are not capable of showing empathy to other beings, regardless if they are humans, androids or animals and when it is proven by the Voigt-Kampff-Empathy Test that the interviewee is an android the bounty hunters have the admission to kill it (Dick 1968, 27).

But there is a contradiction, if humans have the ability to feel empathy why do they only feel empathy with other humans and their pets, real animals as well as electric animals, but not with androids that resemble themselves so much? Deckard seems to be the only human being in the novel that feels empathy with some androids which begins after killing the android Luba Luft (Galvan 1997, 426/427):

> "I'm capable of feeling empathy for at least specific, certain androids. Not for all of them but- one or two. For Luba Luft, as an example, he said to himself."(Dick 2007, 123).

After killing Luba Luft, Rick Deckard's view towards androids changes and he even questions if working as a bounty hunter is the right job for him (Dick 2007, 125). "Rick struggles to come to terms with the humanlike qualities of the androids when retiring them."(Galvan 1997, 418). Deckard also has an affair with the android Rachel Rosen and thinks that "she is as human as any girl he had known" (Galvan 1997, 177). There are more female androids of which Deckard thinks that they are handsome and he also thinks that this is fairly odd that he knows that although they are not human he feels something for them and empathizes with them (Dick 2007, 83). He also wonders whether he is the only person who is emotionally attached to some androids (Dick 2007, 123).

Furthermore, there is a contradiction in the fact that androids have no ability to feel empathy because there are androids in the novel that show empathy (Hayles 1999, 172). One example would be the android Rachel Rosen who is worried about the six androids that escaped and Deckard is instructed to kill (Hayles 1999, 172). According to Hayles (1999, 172), Rachel shows more human feelings apart from empathy, after Deckard killed some friends of hers, she shoves his goat off the roof. She could have done this either out of jealousy of the goat or in revenge for the murder of the androids who were friends of hers (Galvan 1997, 415). In the novel it is said that "An android doesn´t care what happens to another android." (Dick 2007, 88) but the example of Rachel Rosen demonstrates that there are androids who show feelings and care about other androids (Hayles 1999, 172). It also proves that there exist friendships between androids (Galvan 1997, 415). Apart from this example, there are more parts in the novel where androids show human feelings and care about others, for instance, that Rachel is in love with Rick Deckard means that she is able to have feelings for someone and to care about someone: "`I love you`, Rachel said. `If I entered a room and found a sofa covered with your hide I´d score very high on the Voigt-Kampff Test.`" (Dick 2007, 169). So, we can see that Rachel disproves the claim that androids feel no empathy (Galvan 1997, 414) and according to Jabbar (2012) this would mean that if androids are able to feel empathy like humans do, they do not differ from humans.

2.2 The Role of Animals:

Animals, especially pets, play an important role in people´s lives (Huffington 2014). When people own an animal as a pet they usually give it a name and it becomes more like an individual (Beck & Katcher 1996, 11). For many people pets belong to their family (Huffington 2014). There are also many people who talk to their pets like they would talk to a friend and according to a study, 65% of the children that talk to their pets even think that they understand what they are telling them (Beck & Katcher 1996, 14). There was also another study in which 97 participants who have pets were put in situations where they felt social exclusion (Huffington 2014). Shortly after, in order to feel better after being socially excluded, some of the interviewees had to write a text about their best friends, whereas the rest of the interviewees had to write about their pets (Huffington 2014). The outcome of the study has shown that it made no difference if the people wrote about their best friends or their pets, both helped them to feel better (Huffington 2014). Thinking of an animal helped in the same way as thinking of a friend did (Huffington 2014). So animals play a very important role in people's lives in a positive way and are precious to them (Huffington 2014).

Apart from this positive side, there is also a negative side, namely cruelty against animals, for instance, raising animals in factory farms in order to kill them or the killing of seals (Castricano 2008, 286). There is a contradiction; many people in Western countries would consider it a crime to eat, for example, a dog or a cat but they eat other animals that just look differently but feel the same pain cats and dogs would feel (Beck & Katcher 1996). Most people are not conscious of the fact that they love some animals and eat others (Beck & Katcher 1996). So, many people tolerate cruelty towards animals but there are also people who do not, for example, people who are vegetarian and abstain from meat. This whole topic could be discussed in further detail but in order to find a transition to the novel it is important to say that the humans in *Do Androids Dream of Electric Sheep?* do not tolerate any cruelty against animals, as the situations that are given in the Voigt-Kampff Test prove. They regard killing and harming animals as a crime, as the examples of the bullfight, the killing of the lobster and the wasp show (Dick 2007).

Animals play a very important role for the humans in the novel, possessing an animal, either a real one or an electric one, is a sign of wealth, whereat owning real animals is more precious than owning artificial ones (Galvan 1997, 198). Deckard also wishes to have a real animal instead of an electric one:

> "He thought, too, about his need for a real animal; within him an actual hatred once more manifested itself toward his electric sheep, which he had to tend, to care about, as if it lived." (Dick 2007, 36).

Furthermore, Deckard's wife is very happy after her husband buys her a goat and tells her that it is a real animal (Dick 1968, 148). Possessing a real animal means so much to the human beings in the novel that Rick Deckard's wife Iran even says that owning the real goat "cures her depression" and that they do not have to pretend any longer that their sheep is real (Dick 2007, 148). Animals are even so important that Iran insists that her husband keeps his job, in which he earns much money which they need for the goat, although he tells her that he would like to do a different job because he feels empathy for the androids (Dick 2007, 151).

When it comes to the androids, it is said that they feel no empathy towards animals and that they usually do not own an animal because they are not capable of providing for it:

> "In two cases that I know of, andys owned and cared for animals. But it's rare. From what I've been able to learn, it generally fails; the andy is unable to keep the animal alive. Animals require an environment of warmth to flourish."
> (Dick 2007, 113).

The android Rachel Rosen, for instance, also possesses animals such as a raccoon and an owl (Dick 2007, 35). Even the title of the novel refers to the importance of animals; it deals with the question if androids also have the desire to possess animals like humans do and I think if androids intend to be like human beings there is no reason why they should not have the desire to own an animal and I also think that the androids who are able to feel empathy can provide for their animals.

3.Conclusion

In conclusion can be said, that there are some obvious differences between androids and humans in the novel, namely that they are artificially created and not born and that they have a different life cycle without birth, growing up and death. Furthermore it is said that they do not believe in Mercerism like humans do and that they have false memory systems. But apart from these facts I do not think that empathy can be defined as a distinguishing factor between humans and androids. The contradiction lies in the fact that if humans are defined by the ability of feeling empathy, they should also be able to feel empathy for androids and not send bounty hunters after them and except for Deckard there are no humans mentioned in the novel that feel empathy for androids. The second contradiction is that there are androids that are able to feel empathy, for humans as well as for androids, for instance, Rachel Rosen. Animals play an important role for humans and are a symbol of their wealth, but as the example of Rachel Rosen proves, there are also androids that possess animals. I think that empathy, which is tested in the Voight Kampff Test, and the possession of animals are no clear factors to differentiate between human beings and androids. In my opinion the androids feel the same humans do and behave like humans and the only distinguishing factors are the obvious ones I have mentioned above. The lives of the androids are shorter and in some kind different than the ones of the humans but I think that they are as precious as the human's lives and in the end of the novel Rick Deckard believes that "The electric things have their lives, too. Paltry as those lives are." (Dick 2007, 211).

Bibliography

Beck Alan M., Katcher Aaron. *Between Pets and People: The Importance of AnimalCompanionship*. United States: Purdue University Press, 1996. Print.

Bhaba, Homi. *Location of Culture*. New York: Routledge, 1994. Print.

Castricano, Jodey. *Animal Subjects*. Canada: Wilfrid Laurier University Press, 2008. Print.

Dick, Philp K. *Do Androids Dream of Electric Sheep?*. Great Britain: Orion PublishingGroup, 2007. Print.

Galvan, Jill. *Entering the Posthuman Collective in Philip K. Dick´s Do Androids Dream of Electric Sheep?*. Science Fiction Studies 24.3 (Nov, 1997). Web. 22   Oct. 2014.

Hayles, N. Katherina. *How We Became Posthuman: Virtual Bodies in Cybernetics,Literature, and Informatics*. London: University of Chicago Press, 1999. Print.

Huffington Arianna. *On the Importance of Appreciating Animals*. Huffington Post. 13 Jan. 2014. Web. 22 Oct. 2014.

Huit, W. *Empathetic Listening*. Educational Psychology Interactive. Valdosta: Valdosta State University, 2009. Web. 22 Oct. 2014.

Jabbar, Wisam Kh ,Abdul. *Colonial Mimicry om Philip Dick´s Do Androids Dream of Electric Sheep?*. Inquire Journal of Comparative Literature. 2002. Web.   22 Oct. 2014.

Matthews, Cate. *Why Empathy is More Powerful than Sympathy*. Huffington Post. 12 Dec. 2013. Web 22 Oct 2014.

Oxford Advanced Learner´s Dictionary. Oxford: Oxford University Press, 2010. Print.

Oxford Dictionaries. Oxford University Press, 2014. Web. 22 Oct. 2014.

Williams, Yolanda. *What is Empathy?* Education Portal. n.d. Web. 22 Oct. 2014.

BEI GRIN MACHT SICH IHR WISSEN BEZAHLT

- Wir veröffentlichen Ihre Hausarbeit, Bachelor- und Masterarbeit

- Ihr eigenes eBook und Buch - weltweit in allen wichtigen Shops

- Verdienen Sie an jedem Verkauf

Jetzt bei www.GRIN.com hochladen und kostenlos publizieren